THE BOOK OF THE
PIG

THE BOOK OF THE
PIG

words by Jack Denton Scott

photographs by Ozzie Sweet

G. P. PUTNAM'S SONS NEW YORK

Our gratitude to Betty and Clayton Miller
who generously shared their Dundee, New York, farm,
their knowledge and their pigs.

A warm thanks to the good people at the
Snowflake Pig Farm, Snowflake, Arizona, for their very
special help and hospitality.

JDS · OS

Text copyright © 1981 by Jack Denton Scott
Photographs copyright © 1981 by Ozzie Sweet
All rights reserved.
Published simultaneously in Canada by Academic
Press Canada Limited, Toronto.
Printed in the United States of America
First Impression
Book design by Kathleen Westray
Library of Congress Cataloging in Publication Data
Scott, Jack Denton.
The book of the pig.
Summary: Discusses the characteristics
and habits of pigs, their relatives, their history,
and their helpfulness to man.
1. Swine—Juvenile literature. [1. Pigs]
I. Sweet, Ozzie. II. Title.
SF395.5.S38 636.4 80-28386
ISBN 0-399-20718-X

This is dedicated to MARGARET FRITH, our friend and editor who had the idea for this book (and others). Also in appreciation of the long way she has taken this team as the result of her creative ability, editorial sureness, enthusiasm and encouragement.
Nulli secundus!

JACK DENTON SCOTT · OZZIE SWEET

Sheep are in the meadow, cows are in the corn,
Pigs are in the clover and all's right with the morn.

ON the Clayton Miller farm in upstate New York, the pigs really are in clover, which is the farmer's way of saying that life is good.

Piglets roam flower-dappled meadows, sometimes by themselves, sometimes accompanied by their mothers. One large boar always walks to the mailbox with Betty Miller, another comes when called and follows the Millers like a dog.

The farm, not far from Dundee, is set well back off a secondary road, part of its acreage screened by a lush growth of shining pines. Meadows blend into fields, and when the wind comes hurtling off the distant hills the Miller land looks like an ocean rippling in the breeze.

Although there are a few other animals on the farm, including a domestic rabbit that has the run of the place, the main residents are the pigs—lucky pigs that have clean quarters and attentive owners.

The Millers, who dubiously acquired a single pig and watched it grow into a farmful, are properly impressed with the persuasive personalities of pigs. The observation of animal expert Edward Hyams that "Pigs are not only intelligent, they are extremely adaptable and highly emotional, capable of affection for human beings and even of devotion," does not come as news to the Millers.

Like most people who know pigs, the Millers pamper their "pig people," as they call them, seeing that they get the proper inoculations against a dozen or more diseases, watching their weight and caring for them with affection. They do not treat their animals as so many pounds of pork, the way the five-billion-dollar agri-industry does, raising thousands of pigs at a time, pigs that rarely see the sun or a blade of grass. The Millers resent the biological and environmental manipulations of the mass producers, but they do admit that mass production is necessary.

Along with the work, the Millers and their daughter Nancy have found running a pig farm fun and rewarding. They romp with their piglets as they would with puppies, and the little pigs respond with rollicking pleasure. But it isn't only piglets that respond to people. The size of the pig doesn't matter. A person only has to show respect and affection for a pig, and it will respond.

In a small New England village, there is a 1,000 pound sow that wanders amiably through the neighborhood looking for handouts. And she seems to enjoy strolling the shady streets with a considerate companion.

Naturalist F. E. Zeuner puts the pig's attitude of responsiveness to humans in perspective: "The pig is one of those animals psychologically preadapted to domestication. It was so predisposed to cooperate with man that it was domesticated over and over again in a great many different places."

Examples of the pig's adaptability and intelligence abound. One pig was trained by its owner to guard his property while he was away. Another pig, extremely fond of bathing, was quickly taught to pull a chain on a shower rigged up for her. And on the Miller farm some pigs are so cooperative that they actually climb on the scales to be weighed.

Naturalist W. H. Hudson sums up pig intelligence this way: "The pig is not suspicious, or shrinkingly submissive, like horses, cattle and sheep; nor an impudent devil-may-care like the goat; nor hostile like the goose; nor condescending like the cat; nor a flattering parasite like the dog. The pig views us as fellow citizens and brothers, and takes it for granted that we understand his language."

Pigs are superb mothers. One sow with young attacked a tractor that she thought was getting too close and menacing her brood. Another determinedly made her own selection of boar when she was ready to mate. Ignoring the boars on her own farm, she made her way to a farm some distance away, lifting the latches of several gates to get to a particular stud boar housed there.

Usually, though, pig breeding is controlled by the owners. The ideal sire is a strong, healthy, purebred boar with a good disposition and the proven ability to father strong, vigorous pigs. Boars, if well developed, can breed at five to eight months of age, and can mate with from twenty to thirty sows during the first breeding season. Fully grown boars can breed with double that number, and one lusty fellow mated with twenty-four sows in twenty-four hours.

The mother, or sow, should come from a breed that produces good mothers, should have the proper length body, well-developed udders with two rows of teats and at least six teats in each row. Ideally, young females can be mated when they are between six and eight months old. Then the first litter is born when the female is about one year old.

The time when a female can mate and conceive, called the period of estrus, lasts for three days. She is most likely to conceive during the second or third day, but if the mating doesn't take, she will be ready for mating again in three weeks, and every three weeks after that until she conceives.

Before the female settles down to mate, she usually runs from the boar. He follows persistently, grunting, and occasionally foaming at the mouth. Sometimes there is a comic mock fight, the male pretending to bite the female's ears and neck.

Often the female will reject one attentive male and then almost immediately accept another. She signals that she is ready by abruptly halting during the chase, arching her back and cocking her ears. Frequently, the pair then move around one another, brushing sides and touching noses. Finally, they join in a strangely motionless union that may last for six minutes.

Often after the mating, the two lie side by side, heads together and if left alone they will remain together for some time, ignoring all other pigs in the area.

(18)

Healthy adult females can have two litters a year, each time giving birth to, or farrowing, anywhere from eight to twelve piglets, with eight or nine an average number. The record litter numbered thirty-four.

Following a 112-day gestation period, a normal birthing is swift, each of the newborn easily sliding from its mother, each wet, eyes closed, bodies slicked back seallike. Soon after, a well-cared-for litter will be attended by the farmer or breeder who will clip the umbilical cords from the piglets and cut off the two sharp "needle," or "wolf," teeth. These tiny teeth not only can grow into tusks (a throwback to wild boar ancestors) but also could damage the mother's teats as the young nurse.

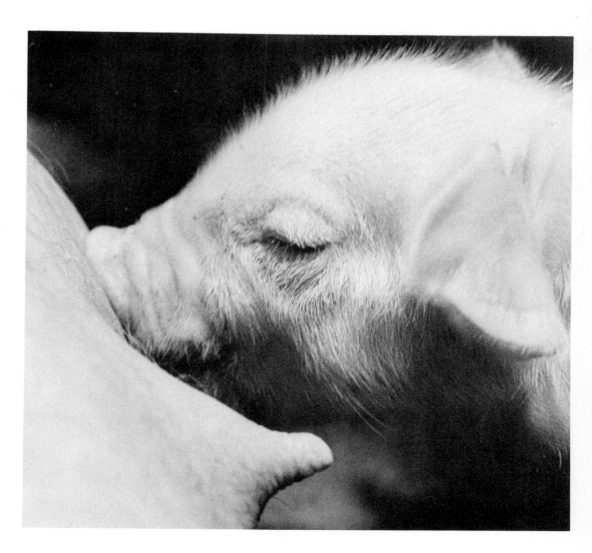

As quickly as possible each piglet goes to one of its mother's teats, establishing a claim it will fight to keep as long as it is nursing. The piglets will nurse several times daily, or as often as the sow will permit it, and will consume about 8 quarts of protein-rich milk in twenty-four hours, the mother often uttering a cooing or purring sound as they nurse.

Only minutes after birth the 2½- to 3-pound offspring are romping around. Scientists claim that the piglets' mobility is equivalent to that of a 2½-year-old child.

Not long after the first feeding, the little pigs which seem to be born already housebroken, find their way to a far corner of the farrowing, or birthing, pen, which they will automatically use as their toilet. The mother of course does the same thing: cleanliness seems to come naturally to pigs.

The piglets depend completely upon their mother's milk for three weeks. After that period, although they still nurse from time to time, they look for other food and copy what their mother does when she takes them out in the field. When she roots with her tough snout, they do the same thing with their tender pink ones, sometimes finding grubs, snails, worms, various insects, or tender plant roots. They learn at an early age that just about anything is good to eat.

The period when the youngsters are weaned away from nursing varies from six to ten weeks after birth, the time often depending upon the mother. Some sows will let their young nurse for the full ten weeks, others will begin to forcibly wean them at the earlier date.

Even though they are fed regularly by the farmer or breeder, the youngsters, ranging the fields together as a litter, trailing along behind mother, will still forage for themselves, rooting, grazing, walking carefully in tall grass, rushing eagerly across open meadows, resting in the sun or shade, lying in the meadow, ears up, like a bunch of bunnies.

Though the piglets are weaned, they still seek the protection and comfort of their mother and will do so for at least another two months. At that age their adult character starts to assert itself. The boars begin to assume their proud, aloof, almost regal airs, retaining these traits of their wild boar forebears. The females are gentler, less likely to fight with one another, more sociable.

Young pigs can almost be seen growing right before your eyes. It has been scientifically proved that pigs grow more rapidly than any other farm animal; 400 pounds of feed produces 100 pounds of body weight. By the time the piglets are weaned, they have increased their weight more than ten times, to about 35 pounds. In just six months those youngsters that weighed 3 pounds at birth will increase their weight by about seven thousand percent, to 220 pounds. If left to grow to adulthood, an average pig will weigh about 800 pounds, the record weight being 1,904 pounds.

After they are weaned and have grown to weigh 100 pounds or more, pigs are classified. Before that they are *piglets*, or *suckling pigs*. A youngster, of either sex, under 120 pounds is called a *pig*, or a *shoat*. A larger animal, of either sex, over 120 pounds, is a *hog*. A *boar* is a male used for breeding. A *sow* is a female that has produced one litter and is used for breeding. A female that has not yet produced a litter is a *gilt*. A male, raised for market and castrated when young, is a *barrow*. A castrated male that has reached the breeding age is a *stag*.

But, as the Clayton Millers discovered, raising pigs is not simply a matter of standard classifications and farmyard routine. Pigs have their own ideas. One of the Millers' nearly full-grown boars, Andy, didn't like being alone. He preferred to have a piglet for company.

One sow and her litter were always locked in the farrowing pen while her brood was nursing. The gate of the pen was latched, but Andy had no trouble unlatching it and summoning one piglet, the runt of the litter, a feisty little fellow the Millers named "Sawyer."

Every morning Andy would unlatch the gate, and he and Sawyer would saunter off into the fields. Believing that the piglet was better off with its mother, the Millers changed the simple latch for a complicated one. It didn't work. Andy still took Sawyer for a stroll every day.

It wasn't long before the Millers noted that Sawyer was no longer a runt. The days that he spent in the fields with Andy had fattened him. He was growing faster in the company of Andy than he would have competing with the rest of the litter. Also he was becoming gentler, more tractable. Now he didn't have to be the aggressive runt; no longer did he have to fight the larger piglets in the litter in order to survive.

Was the boar Andy exhibiting pig instinct or pig intellect when he "adopted" Sawyer? We don't know, but a five-year research program at the University of Kentucky found that pigs not only are the smartest of all farm animals, but also are more intelligent than dogs, mastering any trick or feat accomplished by canines in much shorter time.

Pigs have easily been taught to tumble, retrieve, race in competition, pull a cart, dance and scent land mines in a war zone. A female pig in England learned simply by observation to become better at scenting, pointing and retrieving game birds than trained bird dogs.

Someone (probably a goat lover) once said, "Okay, if pigs are so smart why can't they talk?"

They can—among themselves. A scientific study of that language discovered that the sounds that pigs utter are significant. Grunts have been found to mean, "Do as I say." "Watch out!" "Here I am." "Dinner is ready." "Who are you?" "Where are you?" Pigs also grunt with pleasure or with aggression, and have a woeful cry of unhappiness and a shrill distress squeal.

Louis Bromfield, a writer with a love of pigs, claimed, "Among all animals there is none which has such a variety of sounds obviously for the purposes of communication and even gossip as the pig. They have a whole variety of sounds including not only pitch but intonation and actual formation of given sounds."

What else do we know about this extraordinary animal?

The present name "pig" is itself a word of obscure origin, but it is believed that it came from the Low German word *bigge*, the old common name given to domestic swine of any age. According to the *Encyclopaedia Britannica*

The pig belongs to the class Mammalia, or animals possessing teats for suckling their young. . . . Pigs are rotund-bodied, short-legged, artiodactyl (having an even number of toes) animals of omnivorous habits, having thick skin from which grow short, coarse bristles, a long mobile snout, small tail and feet with two functional and two nonfunctional digits. A mature pig has 44 teeth, carries its head low, and eats, drinks and breathes close to the ground.

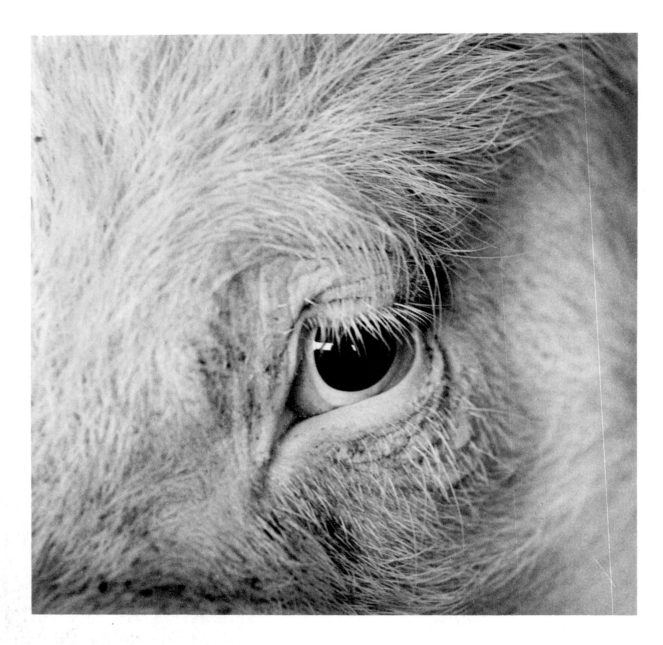

Author Louis Bromfield thought that the most impressive physical attribute of the pig was its eyes. "Whoever has really looked into the eye of a shrewd old sow should feel humility," he wrote. "It is a bright clear eye, more like the eye of a human than the eye of any other animal. It looks at you quite directly, even with what might be called a piercing gaze. The look sizes you up, appraises you."

Most of us, however, consider the pig's snout its most unique feature. Long, reinforced with tough cartilage, yet covered with tiny sensitive pores, it is both an impressive digging tool and scenting organ.

If it weren't for the pig's snout the cuisine of France would be missing its most expensive status item: "Black diamonds," or black truffles, found mainly in the Périgord area. Valued at $200 a pound, truffles grow 12 inches underground, and for many years pigs (only females, called *chercheurs,* "searchers") have been the most adept at finding the precious fungi, which they can scent at 20 feet. The animal also is successfully used to locate the equally expensive white truffles of the Piedmont region in Italy. The variety of truffles makes no difference to the sensitive snout of the pig.

Strangely, truffles, black or white, are found only in France and Italy and nowhere else in the world. It is not known when the first pig was trained to scent truffles, but for as long as memory serves, pigs have been the major truffle-hunters in both countries, and in the truffle regions pigs are held in high esteem by everyone.

Trained dogs are also used to scent truffles, but they can only locate the ripest of them and must cover the ground daily. With super-scenting pigs, once a week is enough.

And truffle-hunting is just one example of porcine usefulness. At Puná Island, Ecuador, the coveted, deeply buried mole crabs are routed out of the sand by specially trained sharp-nosed pigs.

Placed in fields after corn and other crops have been mechanically harvested, pigs, using that remarkable snout for their own benefit, pick up spilled or missed corn as effectively as a vacuum hose. But this mop-up operation benefits us, too, for by removing those

leavings from the fields, the pigs prevent future crop infection and discourage destructive parasites that feed on leftovers from harvests, then attack later crops.

Ancient peoples learned to utilize the pig's snout in yet another way, using the animal in herds as a sort of agricultural machine to bulldoze the forested land and help to clear and prepare it for farming. Rooting relentlessly through the forest, a herd of pigs wiped out the undergrowth, prevented tree regeneration by eating the seeds, acorns, beechnuts, fruits, and also destroyed pests such as mice, slugs and snails.

That versatile snout—its rooter—is, in fact, the physical symbol of the pig. It is claimed by some who know pigs that the animals must root or die. Whether this is fact or fable has not been proven, but it is true that if one watches a pig in a concrete or wooden-floored pen, in sand or sawdust, wood shavings or on hard-beaten earth, this fascinating animal *will* root. Reflex action or necessity? Who knows?

One thing is certain: Rooting produces animal or vegetable food from the earth's larder that is uniquely available to the pig, whose omnivorous appetite is a major part of its survival armor.

Perhaps when rooting in the damp, cool earth the pig's sensitive snout sends cooling messages to its body. We do know that pigs can't sweat through their almost hairless skin and thick layer of subcutaneous fat. While we humans, also with mostly hairless skin, cool ourselves by evaporating as much as 3 ounces of body liquid per hour from each square foot of body surface, a pig barely oozes out $\frac{1}{10}$ ounce per square foot, and this really isn't sweat. Therefore, exposure to direct sunlight and air temperature over 97° F. can be fatal to an adult pig. In order to compensate for this vulnerability to heat, and the inability to sweat, the pig tries to wet its skin with external moisture in an exercise called wallowing.

Pigs like clean wallows, not messy mud holes, favoring a bed of clean, moist earth, preferably after a rain and in a shady place. But if the conditions they prefer aren't available, the instinct to survive will cause them to go to any lengths to get relief—even to using sloppy

mud holes or, if penned and unable to seek a wallow, to the extreme of using their own excreta.

A British study showed that if pigs were penned in temperatures below 84° F., they carefully deposited their excreta away from feeding and sleeping areas. But in heat above 84°, in self-protection, they excreted throughout the pen and attempted to cool themselves by rolling in their own mess.

Pigs have been rooting and wallowing in the earth for a very long time. Paleontologists generally agree that they have been around for about nineteen million years, although there are some who believe they date back as far as thirty-six million years.

We do know that the ancestor of our appealing, clever, useful, present-day pig was the strange-looking prehistoric giant, the tusked hog, *Palaeochoerus,* which eventually evolved into the sleek European wild boar, *Sus scrofa.*

The aggressive wild boar roamed throughout Europe to Central Asia where it evolved into a smaller subspecies, the Asiatic wild boar, *Sus cristatus.* This boar populated China, India, Ceylon, Thailand and other Asian countries. (Today the original European wild boar can still be found in some remote parts of Europe.)

Wild boars lived near forests and mountains. They roamed in herds that consisted mainly of females and their young, led by an older sow. The mature males usually stayed apart from these herds, although they ranged nearby to protect them if necessary. These wild boars were sociable animals, maintaining close family ties. They were highly intelligent and would vigorously defend family and territory. Some of these admirable traits have passed down to the domestic pig as we know it today. Actually, the pig has undergone fewer evolutionary changes than any other domestic animal, proving that whenever and wherever it evolved, it evolved well for survival.

Other interesting relatives of our pig are in the family *Suidae:* the 6-foot long Bornean Pig, the 1-foot high Pygmy Boar of the Himalayas; the black, pony-sized Forest Hog of equatorial Africa; the ugly African Wart Hog with misshapen head and warted cheeks; and the Red River Hog, or African Bush Pig.

The domestication of the pig probably began when early people stopped moving about and began to settle in one place, although anthropologists note that 10,000 years ago people in the Neolithic Age, the latest period in the Stone Age, had herds of semidomesticated pigs. However, the progression from wild boar to domesticated pig obviously happened in stages and it requires some educated guessing for us to reconstruct the pig's history.

Fifteen thousand years ago Cro-Magnon man painted images of wild boars on cave ceilings at Altamira, Spain. Evolutionist Charles Darwin believed that the Chinese domesticated the pig in 5000 B.C. Remains of domesticated pigs dating back to 6500 B.C. have since been found in Russian Turkestan, and bones unearthed in Mesopotamia prove that farmers were keeping pigs in 3500 B.C. There is some evidence that domesticated pigs existed in Hungary as early as 2500–2400 B.C. and in Egypt before 2500 B.C.

And we know that peoples from ancient times were fascinated by the pig's profile and personality. Replicas of pigs thousands of years old have been found fashioned in Chinese jade, Egyptian ebony, Roman bronze, gold and ivory. An ivory figurine of an appealing, fat, domesticated pig, dated between 2700 B.C. and 2500 B.C., was excavated from a site in Sumer, and a Greek vase dated at 2500 B.C. shows a pair of young pigs touching noses. Artifacts found in Egypt, Greece, Italy and Syria show that peoples of these lands even worshipped the pig at various times and for various reasons; sometimes it represented evil, sometimes good.

Columbus, on his second voyage, brought the first pigs to the New World in 1493, releasing eight of them in Haiti. These pigs reproduced rapidly, their descendants eventually being spread throughout most of the West Indies.

Colonists from Europe also brought pigs. Four pigs taken to the Virginia Colony in 1607 grew to sixty in two years. Their ability to multiply rapidly, endure hardships and their flexible diet made pigs almost as much a factor for the growth of our country as those early pilgrims. Pigs were the source of pork, lard, salted fatback, bacon and hams—much more nourishment than any other animal, domestic or wild, could provide.

In the early 1800s pigs went with the pioneers as they moved west along the Cumberland Trail, trekking through Kentucky, Tennessee, Ohio, Indiana, Illinois and up the wide Mississippi Valley. Later, special "hog drovers," rugged men who guided up to 5,000 animals on a drive, moved them as much as 1,000 miles from frontier farms to the newly forming eastern cities.

In 1810, about 150,000 pigs were driven across rough trails from Kentucky and Ohio to the new cities along the coast in less than a year. By 1840, a single county, Worcester, in Massachusetts, was

supplying Boston alone with two million pounds of pork annually. Pigs sustained America while it was growing, and kept it going during the lean years.

That the animals were able to survive the primitive conditions, and the long, hard herd drives over forest trails and mountain terrain was perhaps in no small measure due to their tough, hardy, wild boar ancestry. Over 300 breeds of domesticated pigs were evolved from those original wild boars of Europe and Asia. All differed from their wild ancestors, and differed among themselves, in color, general conformation, size and disposition. Each breed was developed to meet certain geographical conditions and to satisfy various economic needs.

Probably the most important advance in the development of the domestic pig occurred in England in 1760 when Robert Bakewell of Leicestershire crossed the smaller Chinese pig with the larger, rangier pig of the West. That cross produced a very fat pig at a time when fat was thought to be necessary for tenderness of meat and for marketability.

Today, however, few really fat pigs go to market. Excess fat is not considered desirable either commercially or for the health of the pig. The aim is to produce the 220-pound "feeder" market pig, with its weight mostly lean meat and not the former overweight, sausage, salt pork, and lard pig.

As ways to improve pig breeding and establish pure breeds, herd records were started late in the eighteenth century and pig shows were begun which gained in popularity in the nineteenth century. Pig-breeder associations arose, which registered the pedigrees of pure-bred pigs. Now all these are considered necessary controls to firmly fix good types and define proper breed characteristics in order to protect the purity of breeding stock as well as the interests of purchasers of purebred pigs.

These pure, pedigreed pigs, not crossbreeds, are most popular at fairs, 4-H Club and other shows, and continue to win most of the blue and purple ribbons.

A pig's pedigree is similar to a human's family tree. Although the record of a pedigreed pig's ancestry may go back to the beginning of the breed's history, it is more likely for practical showing and judging purposes to include only three or four previous generations.

As long as the pig is with a person it knows, it takes the show circuit in its stride, cooperating, holding still for many an indignity—close scrutiny of eyes, ears, teeth—even pacing on command. But pigs will not tolerate rough or inconsiderate treatment from anyone.

Today's purebred pig, as shows prove and judges can attest, isn't just any pig. It is a very special animal. Breeders in the United States

have favored and assisted in developing some of the popular, registered pure breeds.

Berkshire. This medium-size black pig, with touches of white on its face, legs and the tip of its tail, is one of the oldest breeds. It originated in Berkshire, England, in 1789 and came to this country in 1823. Berkshires mature early and are considered sound pigs and good breeders, although they are not as prolific as some other breeds. Often boars are used for crossbreeding.

Chester White. White with pink skin, this quiet-natured, adaptable pig which represents a mixture of English types originated in Chester County, Pennsylvania, in the early nineteenth century. Considered an above-average pig, it is a good grazer, matures early, is prolific, and a good mother.

Duroc. This large red represents a cross of Jersey Reds with pigs from Saratoga and Washington counties in New York. The breed was named by Isaac Frink, of Milton, New York, after a stallion owned by the man from whom Frink bought two red pigs in 1823.

Durocs are a popular breed because they possess many qualities that breeders look for in a pig: intelligence, good back, depth of body. They are good grazers, hardy and prolific.

Hampshire. Hampshires were developed in Hampshire, England, and have been established in the United States for 150 years. They are black with a white belt that encircles their shoulders and both forelegs. They cross well with other types of pigs and make excellent mothers. They are popular for lean meat.

Landrace. Developed in Denmark, these pigs are popular in Europe and the United States, where they were first bred in the 1950s. They are noted for length, depth and smoothness of body. White, pink skinned, they are famous for producing superb bacon and hams, long the "secret" of those superior Danish products. The original "ham what am" pig.

Poland China. This popular all-American pig was so named because an early breeder was of Polish ancestry and because some of the first successful litters came from a sow called Old China. It is black with white extremities and is considered one of the best market pigs.

Spotted Poland China. This pig was given vigor by crossbreeding the Poland China with Gloucester Old Spots, imported from England in 1914. Spotted with white or white and black, this large, longer-eared, hardy, prolific breed is considered an excellent commercial pig.

Tamworth. One of the oldest and purest of all breeds, this pig originated in England early in the eighteenth century. Red in color, it is an excellent bacon pig, with a maximum of lean meat on a long, deep-sided body. It is a good breeder and grazer.

Yorkshire. An English pig, this is perhaps the most popular breed of all. It is white, pink skinned, with a very long body. It is noted for the quality of its bacon and loins. Yorkshires make exceptionally good mothers and they produce the largest litters; boars are excellent crossbreeders.

Crossbreeding began to dominate the U.S. pig world in 1936 with the successful union of a Danish Landrace and a British Tamworth. The Landrace was noted for its quality of meat; the Tamworth for its ability to farrow and raise large litters. The offspring, although both boar and sow were purebred in their own breeds, could not be considered for registration as purebred pedigreed pigs.

Today, registered breeds are not often seen in the marketplace; the important function of purebred pigs is to provide a good, proven genetic stock for successful crossbreeding to produce young of exceptional quality, health and vigor. Breeders of pigs learned this technique of combining the best from each pure breed from the raisers of hybrid corn, who experimented until they came up with a winner.

All of this experimentation was essentially for one purpose: to produce more food economically. Seventy-five million pigs go to market in the United States yearly. The percentage of food obtained from the pig exceeds that from any other animal, and the farmer's saying, "We use everything but the grunt," is not too exaggerated. Sixty-five percent of the pig is processed as food; the remainder makes more than 500 other products possible—everything from a bacteria-destroyer to a wood glue.

But the pig does much more for us than feed us and provide us with many useful products. The animal has a digestive system similar to ours and eating habits, blood, teeth and skin that somewhat approximate ours. Hence, medical scientists have obtained from the pig chemical and glandular concentrations that have been used most successfully in treating human diseases: ACTH, a pituitary gland extract used to reduce the pain of arthritis and treat leukemia and rheumatic fever; thyroxine to aid malfunctioning thyroids; insulin for diabetes; heparin to prevent dangerous blood clots.

More than sixty thousand people are alive today because of implanted heart valves taken from pigs and mounted in circular stainless-steel-and-Dacron frames. This device (made possible only by the similarity of pig and human tissue) virtually eliminates blood clotting problems which occur too often with mechanical artificial valves.

Even the pig's skin can be used by doctors to help us. When placed over burned tissue, it relieves the pain of burn-exposed flesh and becomes a second skin until the burned surface grows back. Because it adheres without adhesive, it can be peeled off painlessly.

Pigs are the only other animal besides humans that will voluntarily drink alcohol, so they have been used for a scientific study of alcoholism. Some of the test animals cooperated by eagerly drinking a quart of vodka a day.

At Arizona State University, scientists conducting a study of the effects of jogging and high-fat diets on various heart problems selected eighteen pigs for the program because of their humanlike psychological characteristics, their susceptibility to emotional stress, heart attacks and ulcers.

A test was designed in which some pigs jogged 2 miles a day, and some did not jog at all. The pigs that jogged cooperated for the first lap, but needed encouragement to complete the run—not unlike some human runners when they first start jogging. The researchers found that the jogging pigs appeared more energetic, good-tempered and healthier than the sedentary pigs.

But in spite of all the ways in which the pig has benefited us, old misconceptions still persist. Leading among them are the notions that pigs are dirty and greedy.

Given the opportunity, pigs are naturally among the cleanest of all animals, and the pig is one of the very few animals that will not overeat. Horses, cattle, even dogs will overeat, sometimes to the point of death. But not pigs. They may eat often, but they never eat too much. Pigs have an instinct-controlled appetite.

And they are particular. In one scientific experiment pigs were offered over 200 different vegetables. They refused 171. "When offered variety," the research report concluded, "the pigs rejected the worst, selecting only the best."

(59)

Author George Orwell was thinking clearly when he made pigs the leaders in the farmyard revolution against humans in his novel *Animal Farm*. For, as Napoleon, leader of the pigs and dictator of the farm animals, says, "All animals are equal. But some animals are more equal than others."

That description of a pig has yet to be bettered.

Yet, as aristocrats of the farmyard, second in intellect there only to humans, pigs are normally good-natured social creatures mingling easily and cooperatively with other domestic animals and birds. Young pigs may run into trouble occasionally if they dip their snouts into food belonging to barnyard geese, but otherwise, be it with dog, duck, goat, chicken or man, the pig programs itself pleasantly into any situation.

The more we learn about this remarkable animal the m[...] understand one indisputable fact: Pig is a beautiful word.

Whether it's a contented sow dozing, a big gentle-eyed boa[...] thoughtfully munching grass, a pair of handsome show-stoppers being spruced up for showtime, or piglets diligently learning to root or cavorting merrily in the sun, the overwhelming conclusion is that pigs are pleasing. The earth would be poorer in so many ways without them.